Family is a way
of holding hands
with forever!

Remember This my Children

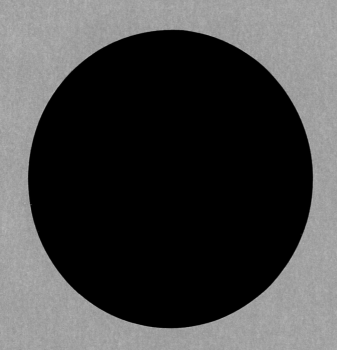

NOAH benSHEA

MAXIT PUBLISHING

Remember This my Children

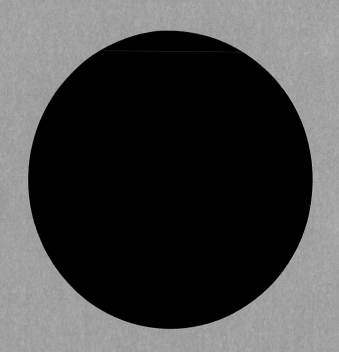

NOAH BEN SHEA

Maxit Publishing

DEDICATION

My heart swells. My daughter graduated from university a week

ago. And my son enters college this year. I'm a guy wrapping up the

twentieth century and my children are already unwrapping the new millennium.

Thinking on their getting older, thinking they might need help more than

they'll want it, I thought it might be appropriate to give them some advice,

some things it has taken my life time to learn and write. Like most of us

when we give advice, we can't be sure who will listen though

inevitably there is something that we need to hear.

So here goes, like time went.

To you who I love as life itself,

here is my legacy.

NOAH BENSHEA

REMEMBER
THIS MY
CHILDREN...

Family is
a way of
holding hands
with forever

⟨꩜꩜꩜꩜꩜꩜꩜꩜꩜꩜꩜꩜꩜꩜꩜⟩

As you head into the future,
the future will be heading at you.

You will make mistakes.
Try to make new ones.

Faith sees around corners.

Your house must have a door
so you can enter yourself
and a window so you can
see beyond yourself.

At every moment be ready
for wonderful things to happen,
and terrible things to happen,
and nothing to happen,
for all will.

REMEMBER THIS MY CHILDREN...

*Memory often wraps whatever we know,
in what we knew.*

You are not alone. And you are alone.

*Opinions like to keep their own company.
Watch the company you keep.*

*Make sure your wisdom is more than
insightful depression.*

Life is a gift.
Prayer is a
thank-you
note.

❧❧❧❧❧❧❧❧❧❧❧❧❧

The best way to get where you're going

is to be where you are.

Love your work; work at love.

Remember what you need to.
And forget when you need to.

Plant and care for that which you will never reap, and you will reap life's reward.

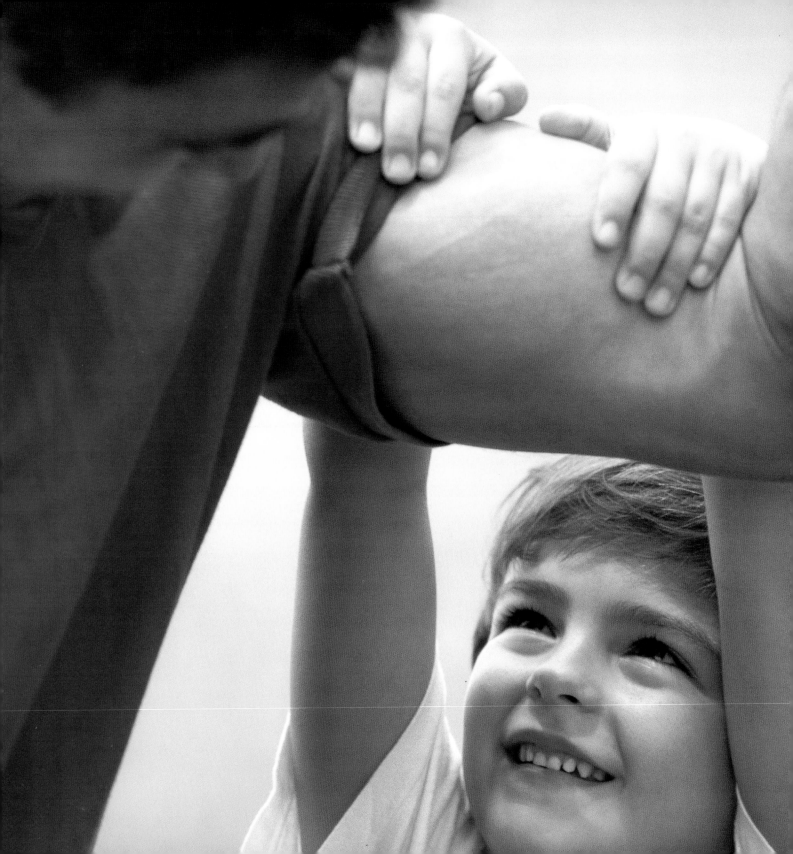

Be cautious of those who confuse kindness with weakness.

REMEMBER THIS MY CHILDREN...

Wisdom is a lot like a parking space.
Sometimes you have to back up to slide into it.

What makes us all blood brothers and sisters
is that we all bleed.

Before you try to change the world,
try improving your neighborhood.

Keep an eye out for the bad guys,
and when you get the chance
remind them to also open their eyes.

*It's the silence
between notes
that makes
the music.*

*O*ne of the best ways to stay warm is to wrap
your arms around someone who is cold.

*Your heart knows what your mind
only thinks it knows.*

Wanting to know about everything is okay; trying everything is not.

*There are all kinds of relationships,
but love should be a relationship that is kind.*

REMEMBER THIS MY CHILDREN...

*All process is not necessarily progress.
All progress is not necessarily painless.*

*The cost of who we are is established by
measuring it against who we might be.*

*It is your right to take what is offered and
your responsibility to give more than you take.*

To lose an old habit, make a new habit.

Prayer is a path where there is none.

ᴪᴪᴪᴪᴪᴪᴪᴪᴪᴪᴪᴪᴪ

A great person is anyone who has
the courage to be a better person.

Gaining altitude often requires only that we lose a bad attitude.

$\mathcal{B}$e a good friend to others,
but always be your own best friend.

*What made the wise men so wise
was the star they chose to follow.
Choose carefully.*

Perfect parents are a contradiction in terms.

REMEMBER THIS MY CHILDREN...

You better like your strengths because
you're going to pay for them.

Over every finish line are the words "begin here."

Pay attention not only to who's important
but also to what's important.

Being right is important;
reminding others you're right is not.

Tears falling on our cheeks can cause us to bloom.

꧁꧁꧁꧁꧁꧁꧁꧁꧁꧁꧁꧁꧁

Experience is a good teacher in life,
but the tuition is your life.

*Anyone who is filled with themselves
can't be increased by others.*

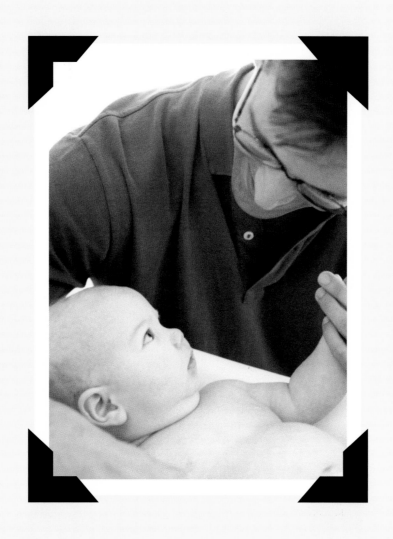

You are a seed containing orchards.

Pray less "please" and more "thank you."

$\mathcal{I}$t's never too late to grow or grow up.

REMEMBER THIS MY CHILDREN...

*Remember to listen to the opinion of others,
but never forget to listen to yourself.*

*Any of us who think our fears are
sleeping are dreaming.*

What does not bend breaks.

*You can climb the highest mountain
if you climb unencumbered by the weight
of your own ego.*

Life can be an unexpected joy. Expect that.

You are strong and vulnerable,
and being vulnerable is a strength.

For everything you grow out of,
there's more you will grow into.

Use the Sabbath as a time out,
a chance to wipe the sweat from your brow,
and see what you are sweating.

The reward for being patient is patience.

Life is more than a performance,
but everyone has to perform their part.

An eternity is any moment
opened with patience.

REMEMBER THIS MY CHILDREN...

*Hold your view as sacred, and see your
blindness as a view on humility.*

*While all of us have to pay penance
there is little reason why we have to pay more.*

*The river doesn't stop flowing because
you've parked your boat for the night.*

*The moments we share with others
make us neighbors in time.*

Put your
faith, not
your fears,
in charge.

Big boys and girls do cry and are often bigger for it.

Choose peace over blessing
because peace is its own blessing and
any blessing that doesn't bring you peace
is no blessing.

*God is common to us all,
but none of us are common to God.*

*Time does not wait for us to learn our lesson
before it moves us on to the next.*

*You can move mountains if you move
one rock at a time.*

REMEMBER THIS MY CHILDREN...

The obvious is often camouflaged by its obviousness.

Understanding is like living in a house where every room has a point of view.

Destiny makes house calls.

Rumination is no less important than imagination.

More paths cross than meet.

Life is a work of art, but it's a work in progress.

❧❧❧❧❧❧❧❧❧❧❧❧❧❧❧

A leader isn't someone who rules over
but lifts up.

*I*t's okay to duck!

Life can be a moving experience
if you allow yourself to be moved
one day at a time.

Your life is not a trial. You are not guilty
for what you can't do.

If you scratch any of us just below
the surface you'll find all of us.

*W*hen you're hungry eat.
When you're done, wash your dish.

REMEMBER THIS MY CHILDREN...

No one can give you their experience of anything
and if they do it is theirs not yours.

Freedom of thought and action also means
you are free to enslave yourself.

Don't complain that others aren't who they once
were but be prepared to accept them for who
they might yet become.

What grows never grows old.

*God is
never so with
you as when
you are alone.*

⁂⁂⁂⁂⁂⁂⁂⁂⁂⁂⁂⁂⁂⁂⁂

*F*ollow the path with a heart.

You can't control other people's emotions
only your response to their emotions.

Kindness is the highest wisdom.

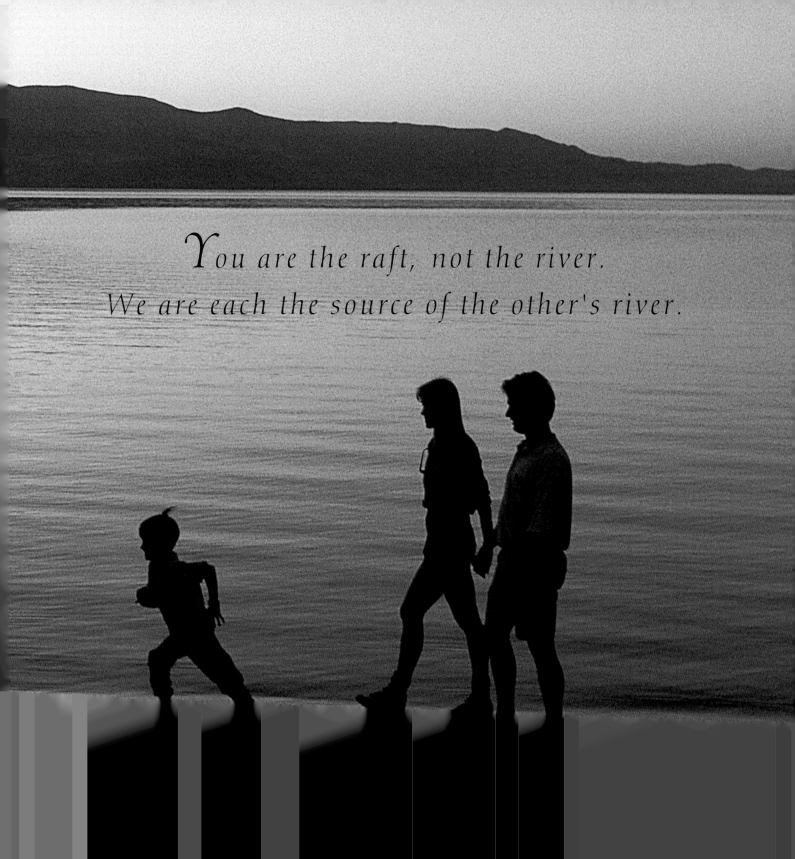

You are the raft, not the river.
We are each the source of the other's river.

The only designer label we all wear says:
"Handmade by God."

*O*nce we sort people by what they do,
we look at them without seeing who they are.

REMEMBER THIS MY CHILDREN...

You know more than you think you know,
and less than you think you know,
and the less you know the more you'll learn.

Do not kiss your children so they will
kiss you back but so they will kiss their children.
And their children's children.

Life does not always ask for volunteers.

Anything worth your doing is worth thinking
about what you're doing.

*It is only
a fool who
has never felt
like one.*

❧❧❧❧❧❧❧❧❧❧❧❧❧❧

In your life you are the paint, the painter, and the painting.

*H*ope for the best, and make peace with the rest.

*A*ll of those who came ahead of you
are cheering for you and will be waiting for you
at the finish line.

Often the best view of life's parade comes from sitting on someone else's shoulders, and a giant is anyone who remembers we are all sitting on someone else's shoulders.

*W*ithout tears there are no rainbows.

Remember your past because it will not pass again.

REMEMBER THIS MY CHILDREN...

*You don't have to be perfect to be loved,
and don't expect perfect love.*

*Anger locks us in our own house and then
burns down the house. Watch for the ashes.*

*A midget is anyone unable to see past
their own opinion.*

*The need to talk with God is a way God
affords us to talk with ourselves.*

Love is a ladder, it lets us climb out of ourselves.

ତ ତ ତ ତ ତ ତ ତ ତ ତ ତ ତ ତ ତ ତ ତ ତ ତ ତ ତ

Reminding others that they make your life richer enriches you.

*L*isten to what others say
and what it says about them.

The reason for faith is not reason.

Growing up is a shifting perspective. First you look up to your parents, then down at them, and then, finally, at them.

Change is the only constant.

*Dare to witness the common
in an uncommon way.*

REMEMBER THIS MY CHILDREN...

Laugh. And at yourself.

*Love yourself when you fail
and you will succeed.*

You have my love across time.

And my blessing.

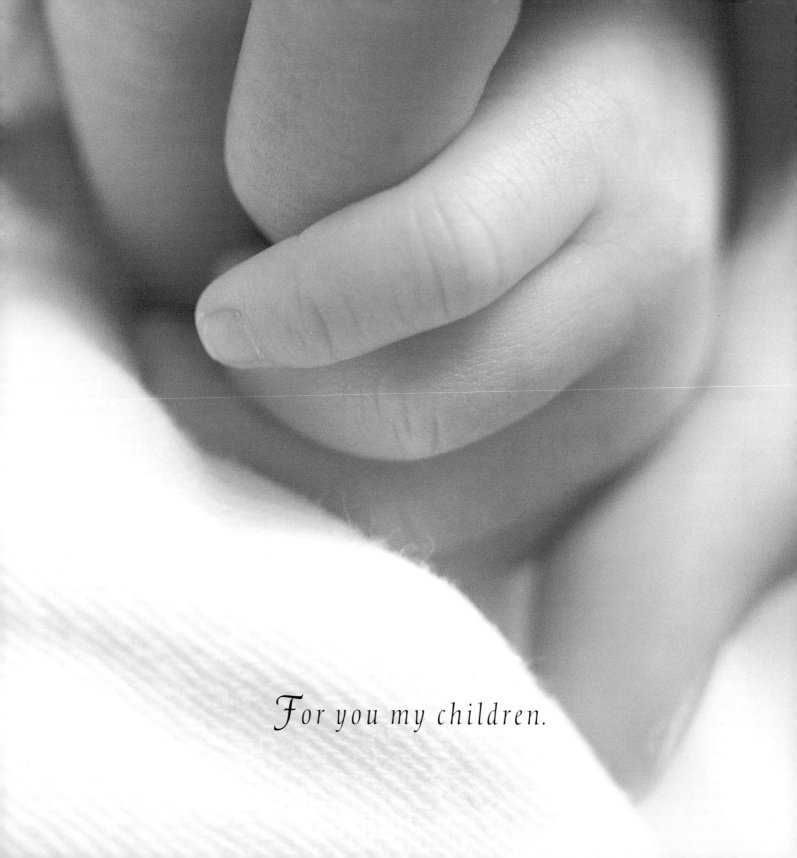

For you my children.

ALSO BY
NOAH benSHEA

Don't Call It Anything

Jacob the Baker

Jacob's Journey

Jacob's Ladder

Great Jewish Quotes

The Word
A spiritual sourcebook

What Every Principal
Would Like To Say...
And What To Say Next Time

Dear Mom

Dear Dad

All books available at
www.noahswindow.com

Library of Congress Cataloging-in-Publication Data

benShea, Noah.
Remember this my children / Noah benShea.1st ed.
p.cm.
ISBN 0-9700174-5-6 (hardcover : alk. paper)
1. Conduct of life. I. Title.
BF637.C5 .B46 2000
170'.44--dc21

00-012355

cover photo ©Brian Pieters/Masterfile

interior photos: EyeWire Images

book design by design©oncepts.(kevinkeller@usa.net)

book production by LeVan Fisher Design.(barbfisher@earthlink.com)